Published in the UK by Peter
Skillen.
This edition published in 2015.

ISBN-13:
978-1511993418

ISBN-10:
1511993413

The

Process

Peter Skillen

Dedication

I dedicate this Book as always to My beautiful Mother and my beautiful children.

I would like to thank Ed Harris for all his help and designs.
Anyone who I have ever learnt from for without them I would still be trapped in the dark.
My beautiful friend and ever present ear to bend David Reed.
Trevor Palmer for the belief you have showed and continued to show in me.
and many special people who continue to support me on this very special journey we call life.

In the Balearic isles of Spain, it is said there is a fountain of inspiration that lives in the heart of a beautiful stone statue of a woman.

Those lucky enough to see through the stone and into her heart, will release the woman from the confines of her cold dark tomb into the arms of true love, and in exchange this the fountain of inspiration that lays within is bestowed upon them.

I have looked into the heart of this statue and been inspired.

Acknowledgements

I would like to thank the following people for their support:

Prit, Rocky and Barinda. Johnny Mactavish, Jason Hull, Andy Smith, Aunty Mary Wood and Tony Olly. Also thanks to John Skillen Martial Arts and Fitness Centre, Amanda P, Rew, Trenna and Moll French.

I'd especially like to thank all of my followers on Facebook and Twitter.

Foreword

Peter Skillen and I first met through our passion for martial arts. When I say martial arts, I mean the tough hands-on, no-questions-asked approach.

Anyone who has ever fought in this arena automatically has my respect, as it takes a certain amount of courage to put body and mind on the line.

However, when I met Peter, I didn't only meet a very competent martial artist and fighter. I also found in him a man who had had far bigger battles outside of the dojo.

His first book, *The Twelve-Step Warrior*, gives great insight into the author's life and his struggles with addiction, abuse and life itself.

Peter not only has a degree, having studied at Brooksby Melton College; he has what is, in my opinion, the highest degree that any human being can achieve, and that is a degree based on life itself. Here is a man who has been there and most definitely has the T-shirt to prove it.

I believe that we all have a guardian angel, and Peter's angel has done a great job in looking after him, but talk about being tested. His angel must be very special and very tired, as he or she has had to work very hard in guiding Peter.

As in *The Twelve-Step Warrior*, Peter has been very honest in this book in sharing his learnt knowledge and wisdom. Knowledge is knowing and wisdom is doing. Peter has both knowledge and wisdom in abundance. He shares very personal and intimate accounts from his life to help the reader understand and cope with the process of loss.

Loss affects us all, but is rarely discussed in Western society. Peter has the courage to face and discuss loss, and to share how at times it nearly broke him, but also how he dealt with it and what he learnt as a result.

As a fellow writer, I know how hard it is to not only write a book, but to bare your soul in a book. Peter bares his soul, and in having the courage to do so has written a work that will bring comfort to those who read it.

It reassures us that even in the darkest of times there is always hope.

Anthony Somers
Owner of Self Empowerment Academy

Introduction

Like many others, I have suffered loss. This includes the loss of many things. I have had so much that was important to keep, but still I suffered loss.

This book poses the question: what is loss? Then it discusses how we normally cope with it.

It offers a way of coping – different tried and tested ways –that I believe could help you not only cope with your losses, but use them to drive you forward into a new and bright future; a future in which you can attain your goals and achieve your dreams.

But first let me tell you a little about myself and about my own losses.

My Journey

My name is Peter Skillen. I am a man in his forties who lives in the small market town of Loughborough. A few years ago I wrote a book called *The Twelve-Step Warrior*. In that book I talk about the life I used to lead and how I suffered many losses; losses I believed I would never get over. I was a drunk and a depressive; an angry, violent and uneducated drunk.

I believed that most of the losses I suffered back then were caused by outside influences. Everything was caused by everyone else. Until I wrote *The Twelve-Step Warrior*, that is.

When I started to write it, I wanted to tell the world how hard done by I had been. I wanted to show the world it wasn't my fault. I wanted to express how my life had been fucked up because of other people. When I first put pen to paper (or should I say finger to keyboard) the words that spilled out were angry words. I was a very angry man! And I wanted the world to know it.

Every time I wrote, anger fuelled by loss spilled out across the page. And every time I read back what I had written I realised that this wasn't what I really felt. You see, I was looking for excuses. I was looking for someone to blame for the losses the world and everyone in it had forced upon me.

I tried to tell my story in many different styles. I went through various phases of writing in numerous tones. I would write in the style of different authors and from many points of view. I wrote, I read, then I deleted. And each time I would leave my computer screen angrier than when I had sat down to write.

Fuck it, I thought. *Who the fuck do you think you are? Who the fuck wants to read your story anyway?* I would delete the file and promise myself that I wouldn't try to write another word. I felt useless. I felt it was all a waste of time.

Why bother? I told myself. *Why, oh why, do I bother?*

After many attempts of going through this process, I realised something. The process I was going through was exactly what I needed to go through. Little did I know it then, but what was happening needed to happen. I was filtering through all the shit I had built up in my life. I realised I was finding my voice, my real voice; the voice that had been trapped for so long behind a veil of anger and shame.

It was only after I had gone through this process that I understood that, in order to tell the world my story, I couldn't use someone else's style. I couldn't use someone else's tone and I couldn't write like other authors. I had to write like me. I had to tell the truth. I had to let go of the anger that had smouldered for years on end beneath the surface of my skin like burning hot larva; a burning that I soon realised burnt no one but me. I had to tell the truth. After all, it is the truth that sets us free.

Understanding the processes I had been through while trying to write *The Twelve-Step Warrior*, I once again sat down to write. But this time I took away the anger, the shame and the blame and replaced these emotions with the truth.

The moment I accepted responsibility for my own life, actions and shortcomings, the words began to flow. And the more I wrote the more open I became.

I wrote about my early life and how I had loved the closeness of my family home. I wrote about how good life had been and how loved I had felt by my large, caring family. I felt happy writing about and remembering the hot, sunny days I had spent with my family and friends, but eventually I hit a point in my young life that was full of shame.

I tried to write it down time and time again, but fear and shame overwhelmed me. The harder I tried, the harder it became, until eventually it broke me. I began to cry. I cried so much that it physically hurt me. I tried to leave my keyboard and walk away, and again the spectre of fear loomed heavy in the air.

I sat with tears streaming down my face. My heart was beating and I was so full of fear; fear of the story I was about to tell. I was about to admit defeat, but then I remembered all the days that had gone before and the feeling of defeat I had felt every other time I had written, read and deleted. It was now or never.

Tentatively, and with tears running down my face, I typed the story of my childhood abuse. The more I typed the more I cried, but I couldn't stop. I seeped tears and typed pain, heartache and shame into every word I wrote. I didn't realise it then, but I know now that I was telling the world about something I had never spoken of before. I was writing and reliving my first account of loss. The loss of my innocence.

As I sat recounting the days of my life, I realised that the more I accepted responsibility for the things I had done wrong and understood the things I had no control over, the freer I became.

Every time I sat down to write I wrote with honesty and a few tears, without shame, for the things that had gone by that I couldn't control. Eventually I got to the point in my book when the bad choices I had started making were my own responsibility. I had to honestly admit to myself that the wrong decisions I had made were mine and mine only.

I recounted the stupid mistakes I had made and the bad choices I had run with. I soon realised that throughout my early adult life I had been a selfish man and I wanted to know why. I wanted to understand why I had made the stupid choices I had made.

I have fathered six beautiful, loving children, who at various times in my life I have let down. I had to know why I had let them down. I had to understand the selfish choices I had made that led to me not being the father I should have been to them.

Through the writing that followed, I started to understand myself. I have to admit that I wasn't a person I really liked. In fact, reading back my story one day I asked myself if I would want me as a friend if I was someone else. The answer was easy; it was a resounding no!

I didn't like the person I was reading about, even though the person I was reading about was myself. Over and over again I asked myself the same question. Why would I want to be friends with a person like this? A selfish, drunk man who thought the sun shone out of his arse and that he was the centre of the universe.

I was an arrogant, self-centred fool who looked out for who I thought was number one: myself. Again, I wanted to press delete, forget about the book and move on.

One day, with fear on my back, listening to the thoughts of self-doubt, I sat down and thought deeply. It came to me like a revelation. In order to confront my fears and finish *The Twelve-Step Warrior*, the warts-and-all story of my dark past, I would have to continue writing. I would have to follow the process; there was no other way.

Day after day, tear after tear, shame after shame, I wrote until my fingers ached and my heart bled. But at the same time something was happening. I was recognising a steady stream throughout the whole process. The feelings of self-doubt and self-pity were dissipating.

I realised that the more I let the feeling flow out through my writing, the freer from the heartaches of the past I was becoming. The process I was going through was becoming cathartic and the more I wrote the lighter I felt. I was actually writing away the fears, anxiety and pains from my past that had haunted me for so long. The more I wrote the better I felt. This spurred me along, and in just a few weeks I had written enough to fill two books.

After the writing was done and all my memories – some that would make the final book and many that would not – were put down in words, I felt euphoric. I had finally written my story.

The following day was not the same. A massive depression hit me and it nearly knocked me off my feet. Why was I so down when I had just managed to achieve a goal I had been working towards for so long? I did what I always do now and analysed why I was feeling so down. I discovered that I was still going through the process. The depression, the euphoria and the tears I had shed while writing *The Twelve-Step Warrior* were all part of the process.

Before I talk about processes, let me first tell you a short story that came to me one night. This particular night I hadn't planned on doing any writing and was trying to relax.

I did what I always do when I want to relax. I dimmed the lights, prepared and lit my small oil burner with water and lavender oil, then found my favourite comfortable throw and laid it out on the sofa. I fluffed two of my cotton pillows, which had that fresh, just-washed smell about them, and positioned them at one end of the sofa.

The room was warm, the air was sweet and my comfortable brown leather sofa was inviting me to take a seat. I laid myself down on the sofa and leant my head on the soft pillows. I was in dreamland almost immediately.

I dreamt I was a man who lived in a faraway land; a land full of warmth and love. I dreamt I was walking through fields and wooded areas, and in my dream I eventually came to the bottom of a lush green mountain. I started to walk to the top of the mountain. Above it the sun shone, and all around me I could hear and see the wild animals that populated this place of astonishing beauty. I felt I was at one with nature.

As I approached the top of the mountain, the sun shone brighter and a feeling of euphoria washed over me. In my dream, I stood bathing in the warmth of the sun, then slowly and gently I opened my eyes and I was back in my dimly candlelit, sweet-smelling room. I slowly sat up, and as I did so I felt this incredible urge to write.

I pulled my laptop out from under the sofa. As I sat there waiting for it to boot up, I thought about what I wanted to write. The only thing that came into my head was the word 'loss'. I felt as if I had been shown a place where my soul was meant to reside; a place of peace.

I sat and thought for a moment about where I was in my life at that time. I drifted into my own mind about how I had thought my life was complete in the context of family. Just a few months earlier I had been living with a girl I loved and four of my beautiful children. I was at university studying for a degree. I had my own martial arts gym and I was working.

Although I might not have shown it the way I should have done, I loved them all from the outer layer of their skin to the deepest part of their souls. But as I sat on my sofa, I thought about how I had lost it all. My world had been torn apart, and the life I had thought I was going to lead had been taken away. The plans I had made and the hard work I was doing to make my family's future free from debt and struggle had been prised out of my grasp, catapulting me into a world of darkness.

I became homeless and closed the gym I had worked so hard to set up. I was no longer working, so the only thing I had left to keep me sane was my university course. I was back signing on at the Jobcentre as I waited for my course to start.

I had been forced out of the house I had made into a home for my family, and I was sleeping rough or sofa surfing at my friends' houses. I wasn't eating properly and my mental state at that time was slowly deteriorating. I was so depressed I would often sit in the alleyway at the side of my old house crying. The pain I felt was worse than anything I had ever experienced before. I felt like a broken man.

I knew that my number-one priority was to stay sober. I clung to one of the greatest phrases I have ever heard: 'This too shall pass.'

The following few months consisted of me sleeping rough and arguing my case with the local council. I was eventually given a small flat. I remember on my first night in the flat that all I had was a sleeping bag and a rucksack full of the few possessions I had left. I lay in a corner on the cold, hard, tiled floor and cried myself to sleep.

Over the next few months I struggled with my emotions, my thoughts and my finances. Close friends and family members helped me with food and often provided a shoulder to cry on. My lifelong friends, Jason Hull and Eamon Keating, were my rocks once again.

When I awoke, I sat up and realised I had to rebuild my life, but it was hard as I was depressed again. *What was I going to do? How could I cope?*

I stayed like this for about a week, in what seemed like an endless cycle of tears and sleep with little food and no interest in what was going on around me. I was in turmoil because I had suffered a great loss.

I was on the edge of insanity, telling myself I would never see my children again; that my ex-partner would try and take them away from me. The spectre of jealousy reared its ugly head every night, telling me that she would meet someone else and that he would be a better father to my children than I had been. Hate and fear ran through my veins. I was fighting a constant battle between love and hate, between truths and untruths, bathed in loneliness and heartbreak.

Something had to be done.
Something had to change. I knew that if I continued like that everything I had built up since leaving the rehabilitation centre ten years previously would be lost.

I decided I had to take control of my life and dig deep. Sitting wallowing in self-pity was not the answer. I had to look back into my past to the place where I had once been lost but had found recovery.

During these months when my life was falling apart, I hadn't been eating. I had neglected my martial arts training and my thoughts were turning towards drink. I contacted Dave, my ever-present AA sponsor. He reminded me of my journey, how far I had come and the cost of going back to my old ways. He listened as I told him how I had fucked it up and how I felt like I was right back at the beginning.

He explained that although I felt as though I was back at the start, I wasn't. I was at a new beginning, but this time, instead of not having a clue where to turn, I had all the tools I needed within my grasp. I had the knowledge of dark days past that I had already championed. And now was the time to use these tools to restart my life.

Dave was right; he normally is. After talking to him I understood that I no longer had nothing. I had my sobriety, I had my university course, I had made great new friends, I was a published author and I had my health, although the latter had dramatically dropped during the previous few months.

I sat down and made a plan. First, I would get myself and my flat in order. It was time to create a new home that my children could visit and where I could continue to live a good life. I awoke the next morning and looked around at what I needed in the flat. I can't lie, it was a cold, soulless place.

I had been given some vouchers by the local council to decorate the place. I chose cool, calming colours, and my old friend from my skinhead days, Dean Baron, came and decorated it for me. Dean is a lovely man and he helped me so much. I'm ever grateful for his help.

After that, the flat looked clean and felt warm. Another friend of mine provided me with carpets that I would pay for over the coming weeks, and my ever-present friend Jason Hull gave me a beautiful sofa. I was so grateful for the friends who helped me get back on my feet. I received my last student grant payment and used it to furnish my flat with kitchen equipment and bedding.

Within a couple of weeks the flat looked and felt like a home. I filled my cupboards with food, bought essential oils and filled my house with positive books, which I read nightly. I went to bed early and got up early. I started training again and continued with my university degree.

I also arranged with my ex-partner to see my children. It was great. There were still arguments and I had issues with what I thought she was doing wrong, but it was her right as a person to live her life her way. She had made the decision that we were not getting back together, so I accepted that and carried on.

I'm not saying it was easy, because it wasn't. It was very hard. Some nights were sleepless, and some days I didn't feel like getting out of bed, but I did. I pushed myself forwards, I listened to positive stories, I watched positive films and programmes, I played a lot of music, and eventually I passed my degree and exceeded my own expectations.

I started to feel grateful that I hadn't stayed on my knees. Instead, I had got back up and fought the demons of the past and kept them at bay. I hadn't realised it until that point, but everything I had learnt since my recovery had come into play. The hours of AA meetings and counselling, my martial arts training and my good friends had led me through this dark time without me turning back to my old ways.

It was at this point as I sat on my comfortable sofa, the air filled with the sweet smell of lavender, that I realised how I had been through all of this before, but this time there was no alcohol to keep me in the pit of self-pity. I had been through the same process that had given me years of heartache and anguish before. This time I had overcome within six months.

When I say overcome, I don't mean that I wasn't still fragile. What I mean is that the process of accepting my situation was quicker than ever before. I knew that acceptance was the key.

I thought about the dream I had just had and the feeling of peace that was within me. I analysed how I had got through this heartbreaking time in my life and had so quickly been able to accept the situation I was in.

I came to the conclusion that this was a process we all have to go through when recovering from our losses. I sat down and wrote what I understood these processes to be. And now I want to share them with you in the hope that recognising these processes may also help you.

What is loss?

Loss occurs when we lose something or someone of great value. Losses come in many guises: it could be the death of a loved one, the loss of a job, or the end of a relationship you thought would last forever. Whatever the loss is, the parting of company between you and something you value can bring you to your knees both physically and emotionally.

Dealing with loss is one of the hardest experiences life has to offer, and when we experience it we often cannot see a way through. Losing your job, losing a relationship or generally losing your way in life can lead to a long-drawn-out time of great sadness and heartache.

I have suffered many losses and been through many dark times, and in these dark times I experienced a broad range of thoughts and emotions. After dealing with loss time after time, I have come to recognise that these long periods of sadness and heartbreak were not as necessary as I thought. I have found that there is a better, more positive, way of dealing with loss. Understanding and finally accepting it for what it is can ultimately become a process of recovery.

But what if you could speed up this process and come to terms with your loss more quickly by dealing with those thoughts and emotions in a different way; a more positive way that in the end would lead to a happier, more productive and more accepting life?

I have found that there is a way to do this. It is based on recognising the processes we go through when dealing with loss, and understanding these as natural processes that lead to healing. These processes are not there to keep us in a place of sadness, but to help us understand them and reach a place of acceptance.

Let me explain…

Loss of a job

Losses come in many different guises, and many are taken more seriously than others. The truth is, it is what is important to the individual that determines the gravity of the losses we suffer. What may not mean much to one person can mean the world to another, so as individuals our losses affect each and every one of us differently. The process of recovery remains the same, but the gravity of the impact depends upon individual circumstances.

My father, for instance, was a hardworking man from a very young age. He was proud to be a hardworking man and proud to support his family. When he lost his last job it hit him like a freight train. My mother tells me, as I was very young at the time, that it hit him so hard that he felt completely useless. This loss of work drew my father into depression and hit his self-esteem so hard that he never recovered. He searched for jobs high and low, but was turned down time after time. Every refusal reduced his self-esteem even further.

My father looked to his friends rather than sharing the pain with his family. In those days, a man was a man and he didn't share his problems. Doing so was seen by many as weakness. Instead, he would take his problems to his friends and his friends went where every man went in those days: to the pub.

In those days, pubs were very male-orientated and women were usually only seen in them on a Friday or Saturday night with their husbands as a weekly treat. During the week, the pub was definitely for the men.

As the job disappointments continued, my father frequented the pub more and more regularly. He was either tying to forget the toil of trying to find work or drowning the sorrows of the day's disappointments.

Due to lack of self-esteem and the onslaught of daily refusals, the job searching stopped before long and the drinking continued until eventually my father gave up. Gone was the hardworking man of the past and in his place stood a man full of anger and regret; a good man, but a shadow of his former self.

Whether male or female, the loss of a job can bring stress, worry and debt, all of which will affect us spiritually and mentally. Who wants to think that they cannot provide for themselves or their family? The thought of not having an income can truly destroy a person's self-esteem; so much so that depression, anxiety and worry will whittle you down until it seems as though there is little hope of ever recovering.

But you *can* recover, and there it is a process to that recovery. The sooner you are able to understand it, the faster the recovery will be.

Loss of a relationship

The loss of a relationship can be so devastating that it literally brings us to our knees. It can fill us with such a crippling feeling of regret, anger or shame that we think we will never recover. Sadly, some people never do.

When we meet someone we are attracted to, it is often because of looks and personality. Having spent time together, the attraction grows until eventually a relationship is formed.

At the beginning, the relationship is full of discovery and wonder. Every little thing our partner does gives us goose pimples, excites us or fills us with laughter.

Who doesn't remember the early days of a relationship: the feeling of anticipation, butterflies and excitement; sitting waiting for the phone to ring or hoping the next message will be from that special person? Then there is the happiness and relief we feel when our new partner arrives for a prearranged date and the ensuing nervousness of how well we are doing on that date. There is the moment before the first kiss and the feeling of joy of getting that "Can we meet again?" message.

Relationships can and should be beautiful experiences that are full of joy and laughter, caring and understanding. I'm not saying that there won't be bad times, because there will, but making up is part of the bonding process that keeps us together. But what happens when that process of making up becomes longer and less fun? What happens if we never make up and the bond is broken?

However, it happens, and whatever the reason it is seldom a happy experience. Something within the relationship happens that breaks the bond.

The worst scenario is when one of the partners within the relationship doesn't see that the relationship is breaking down and that the happiness and laughter has diminished. Sometimes it can be a stupid mistake that has been made on the spur of the moment, or in a moment of madness, that leads to a breaking of the bond forever. How do we cope with this?

Again, it's a process, and not an easy one at that. The ensuing heartache and heartbreak can be so soul-destroying that sadly it has claimed the lives of millions of people throughout history. The pain of a broken relationship is often one of the hardest to bear.

There is a way to mend a broken heart, and it, too, is a process. It's a process of recovery that can take a very long time to recover from, but recognising that it is a process and what that process is can greatly help and ease the feeling of loss we suffer when a relationship breaks down.

Loss of life

If there if one thing we are all certain to experience within our lifetimes it is death. Death is the ultimate loss. Even the thought of losing someone we love causes a searing pain within our souls; so much so that we often avoid even thinking about it. How do we cope with losing a person who is so embroiled in our own lives? What do we do when we know we will never see them alive again?

Death is a certainty for us all, and it is probably the greatest loss we can ever suffer. Sudden death cuts away any possible chance of saying goodbye. The thought of that itself is heart-wrenching in its gravity.

But what about when we know that the death of a loved one is coming and we have time to prepare for it? Does that make it any easier to accept? Sometimes the pain and heartbreak of knowing that our friend, partner, parent or child will be leaving us soon is truly devastating.

Often we take solace in the fact that we had time to prepare and ready ourselves, but in truth are we ever really prepared for the death of someone we love? For the shock, the anger and the regret about the things we should or could have done? Often we punish ourselves for not being there or not doing enough. There is an onslaught of shock, regret and anger, followed by a deep sadness that we think we will never get over.

The truth is with death, we never really do. It's how we react to death and its aftermath that dictates how we feel. There has to be a time of grieving and sometimes, as I have experienced myself, we can be in such terrible shock that this time of grieving can emerge weeks, months or even years later.

My father died some sixteen years before I started writing *The Process*. Although his death brought me to tears, the grief didn't really hit me until months later. In fact, it was six months before I properly entered the grieving stage. This was due to the fact that I was drinking heavily at the time to numb the feelings and emotions I was experiencing.

Eventually, it did happen. The tears flowed and my heart was broken. In wasn't until a year later when I entered the rehabilitation clinic for my own alcohol-related illness that I truly grieved.

I trained my thoughts on what was good. The fact that my father eventually kicked his drinking and spent the last years of his life as a loving father and a doting husband – so much so that he and my mother renewed their vows – helped me to cope with his death.

Another strategy I used was picturing my dad sitting watching over me and thinking about how he would want to see me. Would he want me to be living a depressed, unhappy life full of tears and sadness? Or would he want to look down on a successful, happy man he could be proud of? I like to think it is the second option, and that is exactly why I do what I do.

Someone once asked me if I missed my father. I responded with a resounding "No."

"Why not?" came the reply.

I simply said what I truly believe: "Because he's with me in everything I do and everywhere I go."

As with every other loss, coming to terms with death involves a process. Recognising this process and understanding it will help you come to terms with it and work with it instead of against it.

The Process

Everything has a process. These processes are there for a reason. If the processes are followed, the outcome will always be what it is meant to be. It may not be what we wanted it to be, but it will be what it is meant to be. I have narrowed these processes down to five and in the following chapters I will explain why.

These processes are not anything I have studied, neither do they come from any particular school of thought. These are simply the processes I have found myself going through every time I have suffered loss. I have discovered that when I allow these processes to flow, working through them and with them instead of against them, they always take me to a better place.

These processes are the learning curve of understanding and healing we must go through in order to arrive at the place where we are meant to be.

These processes are not easy and will, without doubt, hurt. They are steeped in pain, drenched in heartache and riddled with anger, but each must be experienced in order to heal mentally, physically and spiritually.

We need to rebuild our lives through process; a process some people never really understand. These next few chapters will help you understand the processes we need to experience in order to heal.

Shock

Often our losses come out of the blue. One minute you are living your life at a steady pace, repeating your normal, everyday routine, when suddenly, like a bolt from the blue, your whole world comes crashing down.

That loss may seem trivial to others, but to you it may feel like the end of the world. You are in shock, and shock can bring with it many different thoughts and emotions.

Suddenly, everything you have ever known – your daily routine, your emotions and all you have ever known in your world – is turned upside down.

Shock can cause all manner of debilitating side effects, such as the literal physical disablement of a human being, causing the body to shut down.

Shock can have a whole manner of side effects, such as:

- Nausea
- Nightmares
- Insomnia
- Flashbacks to the event that caused the shock
- Panic attacks
- Crippling fear
- Loneliness
- Reduced self-esteem
- Feelings of hopelessness
- Deep depression
- Suicidal thoughts

All of these feelings can have far-reaching implications that need to be addressed as soon as they arise. Often we think there is no way out, but, as with everything, there is always a way.

Some of the ways you can counter the effects of shock are listed below.

__Talk about it__

Sharing our losses with other people can greatly reduce the pain and anxiety we feel. A family member or a good friend you trust will sit, listen and let you open up without fear of judgement. Tell them about your emotions. Talk to them about your thoughts and try to get another perspective on the loss you have suffered.

Sometimes when we are in the midst of shock, our thoughts can be overpowering. Feeding these thoughts can quickly debilitate us, taking us into deep depression. If you find that your mood is worsening by the day, it might be worth seeking professional guidance.

Seek professional guidance

While it's always good to share our problems with a family member or friend, sometimes it can be too overwhelming for them. Try as they might, with all the good intentions in the world, your thoughts and emotions can be too much for the strongest of them.

It is at this point that you should turn to someone who is trained in these areas. A good counsellor can help you sift through your thoughts and feelings, and guide you to a place of understanding.

Many people think, as I did, that seeking professional help insinuates that you are some kind of lunatic. This couldn't be further from the truth. You will find that many of the happiest and most successful people in the world from all walks of life, including the business, medical and creative industries, see counsellors. Counsellors are people that should be sought before the onset of madness; they are specialists who can help you come to terms with your loss.

Seek spiritual guidance

Sometimes the shock we suffer affects us more than just physically and mentally; it can hit us deep within our souls. Spiritual counsel can help you in many ways.

Whether you are a person of faith or not, an understanding person of God can guide you through the spiritual rebuilding of your soul. People of faith often turn to their faith leaders and find themselves comforted by that faith. Prayer and meditation can bring calmness and understanding to the most shocking situations.

My own spiritual guidance came from the Christian church.

Keep positive company

Surround yourself with positive people. There is nothing worse than surrounding yourself with people who will misinterpret your thoughts and feelings and feed your negative mindset instead of your positive one. Mix with those who calm and comfort you; people who will listen to you instead of constantly keeping you in a state of shock.

Finally, never come to think that your feelings are too small or insignificant to bother others with. Everyone deals with their emotions in a different way, and what might seem small to others could be the very thing that is tearing you apart inside.

Seek these methods for dealing with shock so that you are able to go through the remaining processes that are necessary to learn, move on and grow in character.

Anger

After the shock of a loss starts to subside, one of the most destructive emotions can take over. Anger is an emotion that can literally kill either you or someone else.

When the red veil of anger falls, we find ourselves reacting in ways that are so out of character that we become unrecognisable.

When under the veil of anger, our actions can be destructive, dangerous and lead to our dark sides revealing themselves in ways we never knew possible.

Uncontrollable anger can lead to the destruction of our own property, destruction of other people's property and even extreme violence. Anger is often the most destructive emotion we experience, and it can cause great loss, especially when it comes to relationships.

How many times have we had an argument with a loved one that really isn't that bad, until eventually one thing is said that causes the red veil to fall? It is then that we find ourselves saying things we would never normally say. The cruellest, most damaging words are said under the red veil.

We may dig deep into the pasts of the ones we love to find the things we know will hurt them most, and what follows is a vomit of hate. Often after an argument or confrontation fuelled by anger, we cannot even remember the hurtful things we have said. The red veil releases the most hateful side of our inner selves. In some extreme cases, anger has led to assaults, extreme violence and even murder.

So how do we deal with anger before it ruins things even more? What we have to understand is that anger is an emotion just like fear, jealousy and love. Anger is not an emotion that should be hidden away. When hidden away, it grows. It simmers deep down inside us, waiting to be triggered by what is often the most trivial of things. Something as trivial as a simple request from someone we love can be the straw that breaks the camel's back.

Anger is an emotion that must have an outlet. You must not allow it to take seed deep inside and fester. Our anger must be challenged and dealt with at the first available opportunity in order for its soul-burning power to be extinguished.

There are many outlets for our anger, and depending on your nature and circumstances at the time, the ways it can be dealt with are many and varied. Some people choose to hit inanimate objects such as walls or doors, but this is a negative outlet because of the damage it can cause.

The actions we must use to dispel anger should be of a positive nature. They must not be harmful to ourselves, other people or property.

Below are some of the tools that can quash our anger and allow other emotions to deal with our losses.

<u>Recognising the triggers</u>

Triggers are the things that bring our anger to the forefront, both mentally and physically. If we recognise these triggers, we can put in place a system that will help us keep anger under control and deal with it in a non-destructive way.

When we understand the things that trigger our anger and feel it rising, we need to learn how to quell these feelings before the red veil falls. But there are also ways to reduce the chance of anger rising.

<u>Dealing with anger when it arises</u>

There are lots of ways we can deal with anger when it rears

its ugly head. Here I have outlined a few of the ways to help immediately quell it:

- If you spot an argument starting, leave the area straightaway. You do not have to stay to make your point valid. Often when we leave the scene of an argument it gives us time to think and to rationalise the subject of the argument. Often it is something very trivial that sparks the almightiest of wars between two people who are otherwise the best of friends.
- Stay calm. Practise deep breathing. Focusing on yourself and the reasons why you are getting angry will help you understand it better. Do not react to potentially volatile situations on the spur of

the moment. Give yourself time to think.

- Weigh up the consequences. Ask yourself: what are the outcomes if I act in anger compared with acting out of reason? You can be sure that a few seconds taken to think the situation through will more often than not subdue your anger and help you respond in a better way to the situation in hand.
- Take responsibility for your own actions. Often we get angry when people are pointing out our faults or that our thoughts, feelings and perspectives on a situation are wrong. But think about this. How many times have you had an argument with a loved one or even a total stranger only to find out that you were the one in

the wrong? If we lash out in anger during an argument, either physically or verbally, the chances of redeeming ourselves greatly diminish. If we take just a little time to ask ourselves: "Is it me? Am I actually wrong? Is it just my ego that's hurt?" we will often find that it is. This allows us to react to the situation in a calm and forthright manner.

- Kill your ego. Your ego is the part of your mind that makes you feel hurt, insulted or deflated, but it also the part of the mind that welcomes praise and feeds your self-esteem. The ego is both good and bad, so like most things there needs to be balance. No one likes their ego to be damaged; it makes us feel many negative emotions, and one of the main ones I have found is anger. On the other hand, no one likes a person whose ego is out of control. It can make us look and sound big-headed or arrogant, causing others to react in ways that could trigger our anger. Ego is something we should be mindful of and keep in check. I've always thought of it as the little imp inside us that is always trying to cause trouble. I try to keep my own little imp in a cage.

Avoiding negative people

Negative people can often fuel the fire of anger. When we are feeling angry, the last thing we need is a negative person reinforcing an emotion that can lead us to negative and destructive behaviour. They are the people who back up our feelings of anger and reinforce our negative actions. They are also the first to flee the scene when our anger is released.

Negative people are those who do not allow you to find the root of your anger. Often the root is not what is standing in front of us or the situation that has arisen. More often than not it is anger that has subsided but still resides within and hasn't been dealt with properly.

Sharing our problems

It has often been said that a problem shared is a problem halved. Based on my own experience, I have to agree. For years I walked around carrying my problems in a metaphysical rucksack on my back. Every problem I had was like a lead brick that I would place in the sack, and eventually it brought me to my knees.

When I entered rehab, I was allowed and encouraged to share my problems with a like-minded, experienced group of people. The moment I started to share my problems, the rucksack felt lighter. It was as if someone was standing behind me, taking them out and throwing them away.

I became lighter and less depressed. The anger I had felt from all the years that had gone before dissipated as the group of people I shared them with listened. They then shared their own experiences, which allowed me to understand the angers that were valid and those that were not.

I don't mind admitting that most of them were not and were of my own making, but some were valid and needed to be aired in order for the power they had over me to be diminished. For me, a problem shared is often a problem dealt with, and when a problem is dealt with the anger it causes is reduced.

You will experience problems throughout your life – we all do – but it is how we deal with these problems that defines whether our reaction is one of anger or one of reason.

Counselling

Sometimes the problems we have feel too big or too heartbreaking, confusing and embarrassing to share with our families, friends or local self-help groups. But these feelings must be aired. We must get these feelings out in the open to enable us to understand them, see them for what they are, and deal with them.

A problem left to fester will often become bigger than it was in the first place. We can create monsters of our small problems that will ruin our lives and create untold amounts of anger and destruction, both within us and without.

When we feel like this, it is advisable to seek professional help. Your local GP or health centre will have the details of many local professional counsellors who specialise in a broad range of areas.

Often we are made to believe that going to see a counsellor is a sign of madness, when in fact going to see a counsellor is a sign of madness prevention. A good counsellor is worth his or her weight in gold. Often a counsellor will open your eyes to a different way of seeing things, which will allow you to control and express

your feelings in a constructive
and non-angry manner.

<u>Physical exercise</u>

Physical exercise releases
endorphins, which create a feel-good
factor, in our brains. So the more
physical exercise we do, coupled with a
good diet, the better we will feel. It
doesn't matter what form of physical
exercise you do as long as it is healthy
and you enjoy it. Sport of all kinds brings
happiness to many people and is a
fantastic tool in combatting anger and
depression.

One of the most positive things we
must understand about our anger is that,
when dealt with in a positive manner, it
can actually be a powerful tool in moving
you through the process to a new
beginning.

When I left rehab, I recognised that I
still had a deep-seated anger. I wasn't
angry at others, but more at myself for
the hurts I had caused and the time I had

wasted. I knew that if I allowed this anger to manifest it would rear its ugly head and ruin any chance I had at true sobriety.

In the past I had trained in martial arts, mainly kickboxing, but I hadn't kept up my training because of my drinking. I decided that getting back into martial arts was the best chance I had at quelling the anger and channelling my energy into something positive.

For me, martial arts was the natural way forward based on the natural fighting streak that had run through my family. My granddad was a boxer and many of my relatives had been fighters.

For you, it could be something like joining a gym, running, fitness classes, athletics or a mixture of sport and any other physical pastime. I would always recommend a physical activity with a goal attached to it, as setting long-term goals coupled with short-term triumphs keeps us focused.

I trained hard on a daily basis and travelled around the country learning from some of the top martial artists available. I attended a number of seminars, courses and training sessions. I achieved multiple belts in different disciplines and turned my negative anger into positive achievement.

When we feel anger building, we need to dispel it quickly and not let it manifest as physical violence. Physical exercise releases natural feel-good endorphins and chemicals in the brain that make us feel better about ourselves and our situations, as well as giving us critical thinking time. Many a problem has been squashed into insignificance after two hours of punching a bag or grappling on the mat.

If the anger inside is not tamed, the next emotion we will discuss can lead to the biggest hurts and regrets imaginable.

<u>Revenge</u>

"A man who seeks revenge must first dig two graves."
(Old Chinese Proverb)

"Revenge is a dish best served cold" is another old saying, but, in actual fact, revenge is a dish that should never be served at all. Believe me, after my experiences I have often thought about revenge. In darker days I have threatened it, and in darker days still I have carried it out. There is nothing more satisfying to an angry person than the thought of revenge and retribution. But as the old Chinese proverb tells us, revenge eventually kills the person who carries it out.

Thoughts of revenge are part of the process that can lead us back to clarity of mind and, believe it or not, back to sanity. If a person merely harbours thoughts of revenge and retribution in the mind, it is generally harmless as long as it is never carried out.

But harbouring such thoughts can cultivate them and keep the mind in a longer state of insanity. The more you cultivate these thoughts, the more likely you are to follow through with the acts of revenge that are infesting your mind. This can result in very harmful and dangerous behaviour.

Acting out revenge is both morally and mentally wrong. It can lead to extreme physical harm and even death: death of the person who the revenge is taken out on, or even death of the person harbouring the thoughts of revenge.

To act out our revenge is to kill ourselves morally, mentally and spiritually. Acting out revenge doesn't solve anything; in fact, it causes more problems. Revenge is almost always acted out a short period of time after the initial incident without thought of consequence, and the ramifications can be massive.

When acted out, revenge is not something that catapults us into a higher regard or station than the person we take our revenge on; rather it lowers us to their level of depravity. Revenge is often regrettable. In hindsight, actions taken in revenge can seem stupid or even dangerous.

There are things that can satisfy the need for revenge other than the act of revenge itself. The act of doing nothing can sometimes be a far more damning act and a far more powerful tool. When we leave a person who has harmed us mentally, physically or spiritually to his or her own thoughts and feelings, this can prove torturous.

Granted, there will be people who do not give two hoots about what you do. These are callous and careless people who do not deserve to live at the same level as us until they have made amends. I am not saying you shouldn't get justice; I am saying acts of revenge have repercussions and consequences that can be very dangerous.

Do people deserve to be brought to justice for their actions? Yes, without doubt! But it has to be done the right way and through the correct channels. When we seek justice and take the appropriate actions, we can achieve peace of mind by knowing that we didn't have to lower ourselves to the perpetrator's level, and we can still have justice.

Revenge is a pathway to more heartache and sorrow. Revenge will eventually eat you up, take away your freedom and blacken your soul. Do not seek revenge. Seek justice if you have to, but seek it through the channels that will not harm you any more than the original act already has.

Realisation

The pain of realisation that all is lost is a hard burden to carry. This pain can be derived from many different places. It can come from the loss of a loved one, the break up of a relationship or marriage, or even the loss of our innocence. This deep-seated pain can lead to depression and anxiety. If this is not dealt with, it can last for years, taking away the happiness we all deserve.

Our pain can manifest itself in a myriad of different ways: mentally, physically and spiritually. Mentally, the anguish and disbelief of what has occurred can be one of the most painful experiences a person can endure. Our imaginations can run riot, developing higher and higher levels of pain as they do. Mental pain hurts us in many ways as it can actually develop into physical pain extremely quickly.

Mental pain will only develop and grow if it is ignored. There is nothing worse than hiding behind a painted smile, making out to the world that everything is fine. The word fine is often used as an acronym for:

Fucked Up
Insecure
Neurotic
Emotional

Fine is neither good nor bad. It exists on a plain somewhere in a state of purgatory; a confusing place of waiting for a cure that will never arrive.

Some say that time is a great healer and I would agree, but there is nothing wrong with giving it a kick up the backside by seeking out help as soon as possible before the descent into physical self-inflicted pain – or worse, death – begins.

Emotional heartbreak can and will, if left to fester, lead to self-inflicted pain that comes in many guises. One of the least understood of all is physical pain.

In my time working as a tutor with vulnerable young people and through meeting many people who have contacted me for help after reading my books, I have witnessed the scars of emotional pain that has turned physical.

Thick, leathered skin layered with bleeding scars on the arm of a sixteen-year-old or the tears of sadness from a once-strong man who has been reduced to a pile of skin and bone kneeling in front of you is not a sight you forget easily. But I believe this type of pain can be avoided if only we understand and trust the process.

Physical and emotional pain can be avoided and are in no way answers to the emotional pain we feel; rather, they are a distraction from the process itself. Rather than dealing with our emotional pain, we often find ways of making it manifest physically in the hope that if we make it a physical reality we can somehow understand it. Self-harm makes complete sense to the individual partaking in the act, but will seem like complete madness to anyone looking on.

My own emotional pain caused by early child abuse manifested itself physically in the form of violence. On more than one occasion I have been needlessly violent for no other reason than that I had pent-up, unchallenged emotional pain.

I make no excuses for any of the violence I have instigated. More often than not there was another way of dealing with it that sadly I never chose. After working with many violent young people, I have found that underneath the iron will and steely shell lies an emotional, hurt and misunderstood person.

This is not to say that there are no bad people in the world, because there are, but the ones I have worked with usually carry with them a story of emotional pain that has been locked away for a very long time.

Physical pain, either self-inflicted or perpetrated against another person, has always, in my experience, led to one thing: spiritual darkness. By this, I mean that the inner soul, the good person we once were, diminishes the further we descend into violence. I have known good men who have been destroyed spiritually because eventually they cannot live with the violence or without it. Either way, they are lost.

I have experienced first-hand the aftermath of violent confrontation; the guilt and worry that seeps into your soul, breaking you down second by second, minute by minute. There is nothing worse than lying awake at night waiting for news that the fight you have just had hasn't killed someone. Or worse, that it has.

Fortunately, I never received the latter, but I know people who have. I have known people both good and bad who have lost their souls and their lives to violence. Unless the emotional pain we experience is tackled and the process of recovery from loss is understood, the consequences are often heartbreaking and even tragic.

I have witnessed good men becoming consumed by violence, both dealt out and self-inflicted. Both types ruined their inner essence: the beautiful, soft, kind, loving people they once were.

I have seen many a man fall into a long life of depression, addiction and loneliness due to a tarnishing of their spirituality. Luckily, I have also witnessed redemption in many cases. Many think there is no way out, but more and more people are starting to understand that there is a way to regain the soul, and that the way to do so is to gain acceptance.

Acceptance

It is only when we accept that loss is part of the process of life itself that we can heal. For years, I carried with me like a rucksack of bricks on my back the pain of loss: loss of innocence through child abuse, loss of love through ignorance, loss of talent through laziness, loss of opportunity through fear, loss of fatherhood through addiction and loss of loved ones through the oldest and often the most hardest loss to deal with: death.

The acceptance of all of these through reason, understanding and process allows us to continue on this sojourn through life. Everything is and has a process. The most important I have found is acceptance.

I have spent years cheating, arguing, lying and making excuses for the most stupid things. And some of the most valued and important things also led to loss, all because I couldn't accept a few simple truths.

Once of the most cutting things a person said to me (although on that occasion I feel it would have been more fitting for the person who said it to have said it to the mirror - there I go, holding on to past hurts and injustices again!) was: "When are you going to take responsibility for your own actions?"

It hurt, and it hurt badly. Not because of the context it was being used in at the time, but because it was so true about almost everything that had happened in my life up to that point. Everything I could control, at least.

Facing up to our own actions, especially when it comes to the loss of a relationship, is one of the biggest steps we can take. No one wants to admit that it might have been them that was at fault. But what if the relationship broke down because of us? Who would want to admit that?

But looking back, I have to admit that ninety percent of the time, the breakups in my life have been my own fault. Either through showing a lack of interest or because of unreliability, lying, jealousy, cheating, lack of respect, addiction or plain old stupidity. When I look back, I realise now that if I had just taken responsibility for my own actions there would have been a lot less heartbreak and a little more laughter.

Death is something we will all experience one day and it can be the hardest of all losses to accept. No one can understand the personal pain that someone feels following the loss of a loved one. I haven't been through this experience many times, but the few times I have were bad enough.

No one, not even I, can explain the feeling of loss when my father died. It's strange really that on the day of his passing I only cried once, and on the day of his funeral I only cried when my two then-estranged daughters, Jade and Amber, arrived.

But in the following months I reached a new depth in my drinking and lost all of my self-worth. I drank copious amounts of alcohol each day and night until I blacked out into unconsciousness.

This continued from the October of my dad's death until March 17th, St Patrick's Day. It was on that day, late at night, that I visited the cemetery and cried a river. I also sat in my mother's arms and cried like a child. My mum talked about all the good times and this helped reinforce memories of my dad, who, after battling his own addictions, overcame them to reveal the gentle, loving father I now remember.

I laughed a lot with my dad during his final years and I remember the good times we had. Even now, as I sit writing this sentence with the hairs on my neck standing on edge, I know he is with me. That is my acceptance.

Confronting what has gone before and making amends where possible has allowed me to accept a life gone by and move on to a peaceful present and an exciting future.

The days of arguments with my ex-partner about trivial things, such as money spent or unspent, and what she did or what I did are long gone. The heartache of love lost with many different women I have met along the way has paled and been replaced by feelings of gratitude and best wishes for their future happiness.

No longer does the pain of jealousy or the worry of losing my children keep me awake at night. Instead, these emotions have been replaced by feelings of peace and compassion. After all, who among us hasn't made a mistake or two in the past?

Once you accept that what is done is done and that it cannot be changed but can be dealt with through process, you will be ready to move on. Remember that everything is a process: from hate to love; from love to heartbreak; and from birth to death. But the sooner we allow ourselves to go through the process the less painful it will be.

Once we have reached a place of acceptance, we can move on. But what do we take with us when we do?

I look back on the people in my life who have come and gone. Some are still with me and sadly others, like my father, have passed away.

I don't carry with me the memories of the bad days, the days that got me down or the days I filled with self-pity, loathing and jealousy. The days of anger and hate are gone. I can honestly say that I hate no one and I know why.

Hate is a killer. It is a twisted emotion that will infest everything that is good and corrupt it. Hate will take away your empathy, your concern and eventually block out any feelings of love.

Jealousy is an emotion that only hurts the person it infects. When we are jealous, the hurt is unavoidable. It kills the vision of anything good in the thing we are jealous of. Our once-beautiful idols – the people of beauty we so doted on – become the very things we despise. Jealousy will make a mockery of the person that holds onto it; not the person it is aimed at. Jealousy is an emotion that can be conquered by letting go.

If we hold on to jealousy towards a person, it eventually consumes us to the point that the person we once were does not exist. We become a dark form of our once-happy selves.

I understand that people can purposely create jealousy within us, but it is up to us to choose whether or not we hold on to it. We first have to ask ourselves: if a person wants me to feel this way, why would I want to be with him or her?

I know how hard it can be to let go of something we cherish, but we have to take a good look at the situation. If the bad outweighs the good, that relationship is heading for certain doom in the long run. It is better to let go now than to suffer greater loss down the line.

I know what you're thinking if you are the jealous type. I also used to think it. You're probably thinking, *Well, if they didn't do the things they do I wouldn't get jealous.*

Try twisting that around for a moment and think about it like this: if I wasn't with the person who made me jealous, I wouldn't feel this way.

If you don't want to feel jealous, maybe you shouldn't mix with those who deliberately want others to feel that way. People who purposely want others to feel jealousy are suffering from the same sort of pain as the person who is the target of their actions. They are insecure in themselves. They are seeking attention. They are seeking self-gratification at the cost of others.

But if they are not doing it deliberately, it is something you have to challenge within yourself. Insecurity, lack of confidence and selflessness (not putting yourself first) can all lead to jealousy. We have to put ourselves first in the beginning as, until we are on the path to healing, we cannot give freely to others unless we are first at peace with ourselves: physically, mentally and emotionally. If we are at peace with ourselves in all these aspects, we will not need to rely on others for our happiness. Instead, we ourselves become the attractors. You cannot become jealous of something you don't need.

I choose, because it is a choice, to remember the good in everything that has gone before and is yet to come. I cannot express the importance of this step enough, but be aware that it is one of the most important steps you must take. Acceptance is key to recovering from loss.

Below are some ideas of how you can use acceptance to deal with loss.

Concentrate on the good

Often when we suffer loss, our thoughts gravitate towards our mistakes and our wrongdoings. Well, the past is the past and we cannot undo what is done. What we can do is concentrate on what was good. Too many times we break ourselves and bring ourselves down because of our mistakes and what we could have done better. Instead, we should try to concentrate on recognising our mistakes and how we can do things differently in the future.

Regret is a heartbreaker and a soul destroyer. As long as we are mindful of our mistakes and challenge ourselves never to make them again, we can cultivate a new beginning. We must refuse to go back to the days of old and kill our inner spirits by going over and over what we should have done. We cannot change it; it is done.

Instead, concentrate on what was good and cultivate that. Feed into the good thoughts and feelings that came before the losses. Don't make the same mistakes again. If we have loved and lost, think about what made it good rather than what made it bad. I'm not saying ignore the bad, I'm saying kill the bad and replace it with the good.

If we have suffered a bereavement of someone we love and someone who loved us, think of it from their point of view. Would they really want you to be unhappy? I doubt that very much. I think that anyone who has passed and who now sits with the angels would want to look down on us and be proud of us. They would want to see us living our lives to the full. They would want us to be happy, leading successful

lives and achieving our dreams,
so they are able to look down on
us with a happy heart knowing
that we are free from pain.
Wouldn't you want that for them?

Cultivate your good emotions

When a farmer sows his
seeds, he sows them on fertile
ground. He sows the seed into
soil that will help the seeds grow
to their full potential. A farmer
doesn't sow his seeds into soil
that will not let them flower. He
gives them the best soil, the best
care and attention, and the very
best feed so that the crop that
grows will be of the very highest
quality.

This is what we should do to
cultivate our good emotions.
Don't throw your good intentions
away. It says in the Bible: "Do
not throw pearls before swine"
(Matthew 7:6). Whether you are a

Christian or not, these are wise words.

I take this to mean, why give your good intentions, ideas or emotions to people who will only shoot them down? What's the point? Your pearls – your thoughts and emotions – need to be cultivated by good feedback, good intentions and a good reward.

The reward in this case is better emotion. You need to feel good about you. It is what is good in you that attracts the good in others. Good thoughts and emotions create peace and happiness. And peace and happiness are all anyone ever truly strives for. These two things will far outweigh any monetary or materialistic ideals.

<u>Get rid of painful reminders</u>

Stop focusing on the things in life that remind you of the bad. You're killing yourself physically, emotionally and spiritually. If you have to, lock them away, but don't dip into them. I have found that it is best to get rid of them, to throw them in the bin. There can be nothing good in keeping anything that reminds us of heartbreak and pain. Throwing them away will be the best thing you ever did.

Replace these items with anything that reminds you of the good times. Surround yourself with happiness, shed the sadness and embrace the happy thoughts these items evoke. No one who has gone from your life would ever want you to feel sad if they truly care about you. You deserve to be happy and you deserve to be at peace.

Practise forgiveness

Forgiveness is the key to accepting what has gone and what will be. Who among us hasn't made a mistake or done something we regret? But if we carry that guilt with us we will never truly be healed.

I have probably made more mistakes than most, and I lived with the regret of those mistakes for many years. Nothing good ever came out of living like that. It burdened me for years, it brought me down and eventually it broke me.

But I eventually learnt forgiveness, and I now practise it in everything I do. You have to start with yourself, and this is one of the hardest things we can do. Why? Because often we don't think we deserve forgiveness for our mistakes.

I'm here to tell you that you do. When we make mistakes, we are often caught up in the throes of anger, jealousy, depression or blind drunkenness. Who wouldn't make a mistake when they are blinded by the darkness these things create? Understand that where you were is not where you are meant or deserve to be. Forgive yourself and move on, but move on without making those same mistakes twice.

Sometimes we are greatly wronged. I was the victim of terrible abuse at the hands of people I knew and trusted. This trust was broken and all it ever brought me was heartache and thoughts of revenge. Until I forgave them, that is.

I thought about them and their battles with their own demons, and how terrible their own lives must have been. I thought about where they must have been and the darkness that must have shrouded them. I was wronged, but carrying it with me only allowed that same darkness to shroud my own life. Instead, I chose forgiveness.

Many will balk at this thought, asking themselves: how can I forgive what has been done? But you can and you should. Not for the saving grace of the perpetrators, but for your own sanity and happiness. I truly believe that a person who carries the burden of another's wrongdoing also carries the other's burdens.

When you forgive, the shroud of darkness will lift and you will be bathed in a light like no other. Their demons will stay with them until they choose to challenge them. And that will be their undoing.

Acceptance can be the longest of all of these processes, but it is without doubt the most fulfilling because acceptance allows you to move forward into a new phase.

We should never live with regret, as the past cannot be changed. Instead, we should learn from our mistakes and cultivate our happiness using what we have learnt from our past experiences to fuel our journeys and speed up the processes we will inevitably face.

The difference now you have read this bookPeter is that you will recognise these thoughts, feelings and emotions for what they are: a natural process.

Trying to skip these processes will only lead to them being drawn out, causing you more pain and distress in the long run. Instead, recognise them, understand them and let them happen. But deal with them proactively and the process will be quicker and lead you to acceptance. You will feel clearer-minded, more knowledgeable, understanding and caring about others and yourself.

After years of heartbreak, anger and unhappiness, I have come to realise that living in this state of unhappiness is one of the cruellest things we can do to ourselves and others. I refuse to believe that any one of us was put on the planet to be unhappy, and so should you.

You are unique, you are one of a kind, and you deserve to live a full and happy life that is rich in kindness and love. Your experiences should not be ones of heartbreak and anger, but of laughter and excitement.

Have fun and cultivate love. Recognise what caused the heartbreaks and the losses of the past, and deal with them in a more positive, fulfilling manner that adds value to your days and nights.

Peter

One day, a friend of mine asked me: "Do you miss your father since he passed away?"

I replied: "No."

"Why?" my friend said.

"Because he is with me everywhere I go."

14848788R00064

Printed in Great Britain
by Amazon.co.uk, Ltd.,
Marston Gate.